CLIMBABLE

CLIMBABLE

Paul Hullah

PARTRIDGE

To order additional copies of this book, contact
Toll Free 800 101 2657 (Singapore)
Toll Free 1 800 81 7340 (Malaysia)
orders.singapore@partridgepublishing.com

www.partridgepublishing.com/singapore

CONTENTS

ABOUT PAUL HULLAH

Veteran of British music and poetry scenes — described by *Sounds* magazine as a 'silver-tongued devil — journalist, academic, and all-round lush', while one of his many unsuccessful bands, Teenage Dog Orgy, was termed 'legendary' by the *NME* — Paul Hullah is currently tenured Associate Professor of British Poetry and Culture at Meiji Gakuin University, Tokyo. Co-founder of *Liberlit*, an international conference forum for 'Discussion and Defence of the Role of Literary Texts in the English Curriculum' <www.liberlit.com>, he has published, presented, and performed internationally in literary studies, EFL, and multimedia poetics. His literary work includes the 'Critical Introduction' to the only officially authorised edition of *Poems by Iris Murdoch*, which he also co-edited (University Education Press, 1997), *Romanticism and Wild Places* (Quadriga Press, 1998), and more recently *We Found Her Hidden: The Remarkable Poetry of Christina Rossetti* (Partridge Books, 2016). He has authored 14 textbooks for English learners in Japan, most featuring 'literary' texts, most often poetry, at their core, and *Rock UK: A Sociocultural History of British Popular Music* (Cengage, 2013). In 2013 he was a recipient of the Asia Pacific Brand Laureate International Personality Award, an honour endorsed by the 4th Prime Minister of Malaysia as well as the country's 13th King. The award citation stated that Hullah was chosen for 'paramount contribution to the cultivation of literature [that has] exceptionally restored the appreciation of poetry and contributed to the literary education of students in Asia.' *Climbable* is his seventh collection of poetry. It follows the award-winning *And Here's What You Could Have Won* (Dionysia Press, 1997), *Let Me Sing My Song* (Dionysia Press, 2000), *Unquenched* (illustrated by Susan Mowatt: Afterdays Press, 2002), *Age's Bullets* (Vagabond Press, 2006), *Homing* (illustrated by Susan Mowatt: Word Power Books, 2011), and *Scenes: Words, Pictures, Music* (with Martin Metcalfe: Word Power Books, 2014), all of which are still available.

<https://www.facebook.com/hullah>

Wendy: It is only the young and innocent that can fly.
Jane: What is young and innocent?
(J. M. Barrie, When Wendy Grew Up)

LET

Let my love go walking with you,
Past the vestry through the voodoo,
Into debris, dirt, detritus, disrepair:
Darkling dawns you do not find me, I am there.

Your fond fabling tune, your friendling,
Through the war-wound to the mending,
Once the silencings subside, let me be heard:
In your closing ways and opening ways, your words.

In your wintering, your raining,
In this bric-a-brac remaining
Of the good that glittered gold but could not stay:
Let my love go walking with you, anyway.

EROICA (ALL GOLDEN AND YOURS)

Imagine us a candyland of carcinogenic dailies,
This rumbled world's ripped time that we have not:
Eclipsed, but peeping through, and heading home,
Eclipsed, but peeping through, and heading home.

Comme la manière noire de ma vie.
Comme si tout n'est pas perdu.

Imagine us a dirt pile final, fortified with failures,
These mounded memories, the end, the rot:
Our testimony dust, but not alone,
Our testimony dust, but not alone.

Comme la manière noire de ma vie.
Comme si tout n'est pas perdu.

Imagine us not knowing love, but seeing love in strangers:
Heroic in our disbeliefs, for what?
These seedling bonds unspoken, fields unsown,
These seedling bonds unspoken, fields unsown.

Comme la manière noire de ma vie.
Comme si tout n'est pas perdu.

THAW

We paint the past so meaningful:
The irony of termini, each ending hypocritical,
That soporific syntax of the sorrows we have seen
Be switched, be slowly soul-cloned
                                    into swaddling swathes serene.

A-stagger through the sadness, fallen frozen:
Sent snow-drunk by the whiteness, rendered snow-blind.
The blizzard storm, her song so long, befuddled me,
Her song so wrong. I could not see. I could not even see.

Hermitic in my igloo heart, sent sightless, sluggish
Sledging over ice-jam floe through frosted field had slewed
And struck me snow-sick: all adrift awhile you
Leave the wintered world to learn it worth returning to.

To learn to gaze on days amazed in rapt autumnal awe,
Refulgent rays renewed through coat to core,
More grateful for the graceful arms that bore
The warless warmth that brought the thought
                                    of thawing thence the thaw.

SONGS OF PRAISE

Maybe there's a moment
In the perigee of wonder,
In the birthing pains of wisdom,
Sapling shoots from treeless tundra.

Myologies of mourning melt
Like snowflakes on a windowsill,
In minding days in songs of praise,
And what would not now will.

Above the fallen full-blown rose
The budding rose joys into view,
The greener grass beyond the gap
Reminding you of you.

Mainly there's a moment
When the harming turns to healing,
As the garden gets to grow again,
This new life becomes a feeling.

BECAUSE OF SHIPS

Launched fifty-score, like arrows,
When first her moonlit Trojan brow
Loomed into view, they sail to you
On hope of who, on hint of how.

The straits and broader sea lines narrow,
Close, and end, as youth has now.
Come rows of ships, come rose-rose lips,
Come tell me who, come teach me how.

HAVISHAM IN SPRINGTIME

'...before I and the world parted.'
(Miss Havisham in Charles Dickens, Great Expectations)

April baby blossom glide,
Fledgling petal suicide
To ground in cherry infancy.

Hasten pilgrim, gaze on this:
The sky is crying dying flowers
In Satis Mansion's rooms and bowers.

Catch them in your mindnet
If you're able, if you're nimble.
Baby-skin pink snowdrifts underfoot.

Annual the burial.
The cherry children
Charnel house.

May morning put her makeup on;
Our love will be not changing so,
Re-solved the puzzle, thus resolved

In still life made of moving paint.
This woman says she wears her tears,
A bridal veil through spinster years,

As if the solid globe had not exploded,
Persuasive as a passion locked and loaded,
Not to hide a sadness but to show that it is real.

We waver, dividing
This day from that night;
We sleep under flowers:
We will be all right.

OLDBORN

Affixing your singspiel to star-
Spangled nightscapes you remake
A wakening day in your image, your image

Of new days undraping, *unheimlich*,
Uncannier now that they mean something
New. For they do. As you do. As we do.

CADENCES OF CLOSENESS

I am singing to the people who are listening. I am singing
To the ones not listening too. They keep their distance; we keep
Cadences of closeness, softer songs that once we knew.
And I've got one for you.

You want a normal hero, uniconic, unByronic,
As a non-platonic tonic — now and then, and next time too —
To these unaesthetic anaesthetic
          afternoons you amble through.
And I've got one for you.

You want white bread with vanilla, perfect pabula of plainness,
An eve all unembellished and a milky *mizu* morning,
An unsequestered steadfast love
          untrammelled, tried and true.
And I've got one for you.

Beat bone-button-neat amid
          the mad chaotic years? I couldn't face
A little life so uneventful:
          now my fucked-up fragments shore against
Your door. No hearts inside
                    this busted vellum deck of fifty-two.
But I've got one for you.

You want an anti-anti-hero, shiny unironic,
Algid coldest catatonic thawed to warming, embryonic,
Like a never lazy Lazarus, not lying, good as new.
And I've got one for you.

You want a softer song than this, a milder melody than mine,
A moment made a monument
                    with symmetry and sense in every line;
Such songs for me are exigent,
                    that mystic music difficult to do.
But I've got one for you.

ETA CARINAE

My vision of love is not new;
If it were I would find a new name
For the lists of the luminous stars
Assailing and assaulting me
Like fires at the edge of the sky
When you and your light years flash by.

My myth of love may have
Its own momentum, make
A minuet inside my musicless mayhem
Where madmen march in with their murder machines
Destroying lake sedges and birds,
Where metal speaks louder than words.

You have to climb over
The evident mountains
And say to yourself,
I deserve this. I want this
Like freemen want nature and music,
Like skies want their luminous stars.

HIKARI (AGE BEFORE BEAUTY)

I was lost inside the darkness,
So I built myself a house there,
And I found myself at home there;
Now I live inside the darkness.

But I dream about the daylight,
As a captive dreams of freedom;
In the darkness of my dwelling
I go dreaming of the daylight.

PORPHYRIA

You told yourself it was too late
Because, in truth, it always was:
From Deor's griefs and jests to these new dirges,
Not meant to mean like battle scars,
                     not meant to mean because.

All things being equal,
Which of course they never are,
We trust the sky, accept the air,
And set our sights not near but rather far,

For smiling stars we swing upon
Are yours and mine alone;
These nightjars croon of moonbeams,
Ours to catch and carry home.

TELEMACHUS

Like Gaudi through cross-haired vainglory,
Your beautifulness and your beauty,
Outreaching like
Daylily petals,
Like oils among rust among metals.

Uncommonest camellia,
Appear and do not disappear,
Re-use the remnant years:
Move forward. Try to tread the trail
That doesn't end in tears.

UNLESS (OF LOVE WE ARE)

Of love we are:
Tight tethered to the passionate,
Unsevered from the kind aorta
Circulating lifeblood seldom spilled,
To pump new moments full of buoyant bliss.

Of love we are:
Attuned attempts to satiate
Our vampire lack as time goes shorter,
Finding us forever unfulfilled,
Unquenched and dry, desiring days like this.

Of love we are:
Descending dusks will wake us late
But not too late to mix the mortar,
Thaumaturgic tears and blood to build
A wall between ourselves and our abyss.

Of love we are:
As welcome wonders replicate
A purer peace as clear as water,
Torn and troubled time is fixed and stilled,
This faith in love condensed into a kiss.

MELOPHOBIA

We made a stony science out of silence,
Recalibrated pauses in the stillness;
Adoring all the animism, abled,
We sprinted through the spirit world like angels.

A blindfolded knife thrower, how I harkened
For the rhythm of the spinning wheel they'd strapped
You to. I thought about the good years too.
I didn't know the outside got so darkened.

So when the moment came I was too weak:
Catching age's bullets twixt my teeth
Was like a cakewalk and a cruise compared to now.
I want to start again; I don't know how.

AIRI

Love is like flying a kite:
It might rise and might not. It might
Soar and soar; might never go. Like lightest
Hope-filled mornings or the darkest frightful night,
But it will do. For me, for you.

Is it spring you'll pick, or
Autumn time, to cancel out our love?
You say you will not tell me? You can't visit me, can't move?
I am wired in this ward in my hospital slippers;
Please come here and carry me home.

She flits, floating by like a stranger,
The herby aroma of newest hydrangea,
Her hair is milk-white but she looks just like you,
As she spooks silent past like the ghosts do.

Black linen, I muse, her white silks tucked beneath,
I watch her wish hard on the same star as me,
Still living like this in the same land as me:
But she is free. But she is free.

POSTULANTS

'It is myself that I remake.'
(W. B. Yeats, 'The Friends That Have It I Do Wrong')

The postulants of loving linger
Lost in silent architecture, not
Of stone, and not of steel, and not of dreams.

They build their house of memories, reside
Behind the rainbow, live beneath the silent streams,
Where no one but a lover comes to call.

The soft substrate of ecstasy
Where pleasure is no foundling but
A property of painless better days

Is where she lives and where she
Lifts me on her stronger silver wings,
Inveigling an innermost nature,
                    a hope from the centre of things.

QUINTESSENCE

for Lou Reid: chanteuse of torch songs, ingénue, star

Wild lament, you acicularis,
Rose and thrown is you and you.
     You the Arctic, you the prairie,
Me the bristling lonesome wood-rose held at home.

You the bloom: your ploidy and your prickle,
You are you and no one else: oldest oldest oldest
Oldest New Year's resolution on its own,

Made in May or made in March or made in June,
Tested well and tested true, then tested new,
But never broken, never spoken, never known.

CAVEATS AND PROLOGUE

Down weirdest days
You waft like wind-song, sweetening streets;
In wayward ways,
Your sweetness wakes the world up:
Your wind-song makes my life complete.

And I'll do that stuff tomorrow: ride
Lung-Ta the wind-horse through this roiling
Reddened snow-cloud rich and ripe with flecks of alga.
And you will be there in the snow-cloud,
For you will be there in the wind.

DAYLIGHTING

For now you have daylight.
Your star must be sleeping,
But not disappearing:
It stays to protect you.

As swiftly comes evening.
Your star reawakens
In new night-dark nearing:
It does not forget you.

LE BROUILLARD

In the leaving of loved ones we look for the wood,
But see trees stand like ghosts where the future once stood,
Sad eyes stare like stains to the heart of the thing,
A summer mendacious to follow no spring.
With a midwinter wind welding ice onto breeze,
And the frost on the bark on the branches of trees.

ANHEDONIA

Дайте мне женщину, бутылку, и шлюпку, и я плаваю прочь.
(Russian saying: 'Give me a woman, a bottle, and a boat, and I sail away.')

A certain sort of silence yours and mine:
The ludic one that lit the latent laughter.

You creep around my coffin
Banging in the final nails.
I cannot change or stop the winds;
I must reset my sails.

A cinnamon dusk with patchouli caresses:
Veridical moments in breezeways we know only after.

You creep around my coffin
Banging in the final nails.
I cannot change or stop the winds;
I must reset my sails.

The only thing we never took was time
Enough to find a silent way to say goodbye.

You creep around my coffin
Banging in the final nails.
I cannot change or stop the winds;
I must reset my sails.

In time we see the truth beyond the lie:
The oldborn truth, the all-forgiving sky.

THE DOUBLE CHLORIDE OF GOLD (FRISSON)

Perimeters of being
Skirt the praxis of this practice
Of abandoning the past or light or both.

Parameters of solace
Hold the baited breath of future failings
Hidden, mob-hand-waiting in your wings.

It's not a fight if no one ever loses;
Through *mauvais foi* and lunacy and strife,
Your humanness and magic murmur mind you:
Should everybody lose, it must be life.

My long-loved cicerone, see me safely,
Grind the gears until the ghosts give up,
Be here and chaperone me to the newlands,
And never leave my side or start to stop.

I love your tiny willingness that leads me,
Like roads despite the quake, the storm, the war:
The turn of your key in my rust-frozen lock,
Frisson as you daintily open the door.

ALFOXDEN

O wrathful wind, awaken women,
Rattle roadway lamps, make children cry.
O holy star celestial
Begin the healing festival,
Reveal the hidden avatar,
Light bringer, show me where we are and why.

Restore the green to fields that long
Lay bare. Restart the life
In leas that grief put there.
The chestnut trees, the wishing
Well, *ma chère*,
My multitasking heart still aches to care.

THE SORT OF YOU

for Paul Reekie (1961-2010)

The last time you beer-hugged me
Midst a fuggy Glasgow booze-a-thon,
You were hurting, hurtling down-
-hill fast, as I was crawling uphill slow.
You told me I was looking old;
I said you looked like sort of you.

The sort of you I love is dancing; ranting
Naked in our cat-shat flophouse hallway,
Hooray-up-she-rises four AM erection,
Shouting swearwords in Old English:
Sparked mad poet jouster cursing at the twilight,
Daring dawn's dreecht daze to take you down.

The sort of you I love is sidling
Past me in the Port of Leith, dependable
Pornography beneath your pristine Harrington, stealthy
Greying night-fox sailing through the crack and ale.
The Reekie wink, the nasal tap, the package palmed:
'Required reading. For later, now,' you said.

Abed, my course set fair for wanking, ripping
Open plain brown wrapper
I came across not only porn, but also poetry:
Your pregnant mind, the zap of zany logic, zip
Of crystal-clarity. You were so fucking good with words.
You were so sort of good, with everything.

The sort of you I love is not this
Sort of you I look for now: absence,
Memory, the would'ves, should've beens,
Conditionals we never knew back then.
Back then, just 'do'.
Just do. Just do. Just *do*.

The week I chanced awake in June of 2010,
You fell asleep in Edinburgh.

Unaware, my kitchen-coma half-corpse
Lazarused to ambulance, intensive care,
Thence padlocked Yokohama ward:
I disappeared in different ways, but I came back.
Resourceful cowardice in me,
Has served me so inventively,
Dead decades of professional escapology.
Defeated by my arrogance and vanity, I come back.
Hindered by huge nothing, you made sure that you could not.

(So many mumbled messages I missed:
Half-heard that you had chosen not to carry on,
Half-dreamed you were no more.
No one dared to tell me you had died
Till they were more than sure that I had not.)

The sort of you I love becomes the part of me
I'm least ashamed of: the better bit that blows and
Bites and bleeds to fly,
To show it's free. To be. To be. To *be*.
We come here not to cuss, condemn, or cry;
We come to sing a lullaby,
A song that might mean why but not goodbye.

O CHILD

Like littlest girls who run with little legs
In driving sleet, and laugh, afraid to fall.
Or littlest boys in summertime
Atop the poplars, never scared to fall.

Your bruised young knees, those tragic trees,
Are portents that the years fulfill:
O child, you don't know painfulness;
You will.

CATALEXIS

To trudge across the treacherous terrain,
As snowflakes turn to sleet that turns to rain,
As ecstasy translates itself to pain,
You love this for the life of you again.

Till sorrow makes a sot of me again,
And madness makes a mess of me again,
And minding makes the most of me again,
I love you for the life of me again.

My heart becomes a singing dove,
Above the purple columbine
And clover, tweeting pleased polari,
Patois, jargon, *ce que ris, verlan*:
"Her love will come and guide you,
And the light will dawn and find you."

ARIA

*(Inspired by and partly based upon the song 'Mon cœur s'ouvre à ta voix'
from Charles-Camille Saint-Saëns' opera Samson and Delilah)*

My spirit opens to your song
Like sun-kissed saponarias in June;
Sing long again, let me lament no more.
Tell me you are coming home, returning soon.

My spirit flies to be with you:
Quicker than an archer's arrow: swift,
A-quiver, emptied, songless,
Gaping for my *tageleid*, thence nevermore to drift.

Sing soft again. Return, refrain
Of tender olden golden pledges, own
Me, fill me up with joy.
Like these fields of wind-blown

Wheat-blades, so my trembling soul
Is shaking, only yearning for your voice
To sing me still, create me choate, whole.
Extend me your aubade; let me rejoice.

MISGIVING

Your lovers will love what they need to and want to,
So you and your sceptical soul opt to roam,
As life leaves you speechless and sulking in silence,
But can you come back? Can you ever come home?

Your love jams like traffic, its taxiing hampered,
Its realness hemmed in by the misguided past
And this misgiving night, but these streetlamps are lighting.
The good lights are lighting at last.

MEZZOTINT

These jumble sale epiphanies
And all the sleep you'll ever need
Will nail you to a cross of fire
And make you weep and plead and bleed.

The baby in the bassinet
Becomes a boorish banished rogue,
As guilt replaces innocence
And hubris whines its broken brogue

Of all the good that would have been
If only time had kinder eyes
To see that love outlasts a life,
As faith outpaces hope. As tides will rise.

GAZEBO BALLERINA

Beneath the teeming tons of rant and rubble,
On cyclones and the silver bells of time,
We sinners search for stepping-stones
                                    in stagnant seas of trouble.

We do not seek to sink or disappear.
I know that you are like that too: I watched you
Dancing naked, in the garden,
                        and the answer seemed so clear.

These morning raindrops rhapsodise our dreams
Of lifelong loves and dances, as, asleep beneath pergolas,
I had seen the world was well designed. Although it seems

That time has stolen everything, that dancer dwells
Inside me, my metaphor
                        placed next to now and then and binding both:
Gazebo ballerina, always here. The silver bells.

LARGER THAN LIFE

Cabin crew, disarm the doors,
A rush of scented non-metallic chalcogen:
Another day diaphanous and new,
The mental jazzy jewellery
Our obdurate old hope,
Invisible and perfect,
Indivisible from you.

Mangosteen and dragonfruit and
Waking through the winter nights
And sleeping through the summer nights
And sleeping through the fancy flights.

Could that be who I think it is?
In language never listened to
But overheard like birdsong riffs
From briars under branches?

And listening beyond the word
We find neglected gardenland,
Where but for smaller margins
You would always be a dancer. We

Must make a song and dance about these pastures new:
I the tune and you gavotting, gamboling, as dancers always do,
And that will make me more than this
And bring me back, and bring me back to you.

BURIED (I LIVE WITH THIS)

Amanuensis, forth we fall
To forge a freer damaged fiefdom:
Falser dawns turned true in fairer ways.

Atheist agnostic, rapt apostle, racked acceptor,
Friar pilgrim postulant and mad forgotten pagan:
Far too many rising roads;
                    far lesser, far too short the finite days.

But all is far from lost while there are mornings.
Dawning wrensong, dawning ringtone, these reminders
Of our silences to break, our sleep to leave:

In syntax all uncertain of
A jumbled maze of *jouissance*,
Love limps into my life again and I forget to breathe.

I live with that, as misers live with gold,
And I am better, glad and young but old,
To live a life so broken yet intact. So harken well,

I hear my Muse, she murmurs soft,
Restrings the silent shamisen,
Sublimest in her summoning, somatic spell

To hymn the stubborn summer time
That stays the sanguine suicides
Beneath this veil of suffering,

Improving perfect circles by erasing them,
And waking me with whispers,
In the silence she will sing:

"Do not weep now, do not worry,
Come and find me, I am buried:
I am buried in a garden. It is spring."

EIDOLON

'...the winter lightning,
Or the waterfall, or music heard so deeply
That it is not heard at all...' (T. S. Eliot, 'The Dry Salvages')

We misremember most things.
I misrecall most certain years:
Fleet youth that rose, sweet crimson wings,
To soar, to stall. To disappear.

These roundabouts and mood swings
Are all that now remains of me:
A head that hurts, a past that stings,
Stale arrogance, spent vanity.

And yet that morning bell still rings,
Sings music wider than the songs
Of younger days, a chime that brings
My heart back home where it belongs.

These calming hopeful homings
Have healed me, held me, moved me more
To misremember everything,
Remake it righter, better than before.

FORGIVENESS AND SLEEP

Have you seen the roses in the rockery that love built
Neath yon gun-metallic sky as never turns to always,
Nothing presupposes more than mockery of strangers,
Sinking into *schadenfreude* to find it as you leave it.

Watchful hills inhabited, our homes and far horizons,
Riverbanks and rivulets and running rills of time gone,
Secret trysts and promises and vigils still for keeping,
Finding of forgiveness from a less saturnine sleeping.

AUTONOMIC LEANDER

Seraphic swimming moonboy see
The unities of drama gape undone:
Half across the Hellespont,
O lithe Leander lost and wont
To drown at saline delta mouth,
Submerged and scared and looking for the lamp.

When summers end, as summers do
Remember that warm evening when she
Took you to her quiet tower and quelled you.
Remember how she held you;
Remember somewhere warmer
Than your lonely seabed grave will be.

O strong Leander,
I have swum through thoughts of you,
I have drowned in dreams of you,
For never once untended, I was never left alone.
Heroic love I knew, when no one fell to ground and
No one died. There are no ghosts. There is
Just me through time and times to tragedy.
This winter storm. This flood. This trysting blood.

GOOD (IN THE AIR)

Good in the air and fair
On the ground, as all around
You Mona Lisas hide in garret
Rooms, and fractured truths rebound:

Chrysanthemum, the golden flower,
Plum blossom on thin kaolin,
The wind and rain. Our territory
Of brilliance: the house our love lives in.

CROOKED

for Martin Metcalfe: il miglior santo fratello

We are the crooked people
And we crawled some crooked miles,
Relocated homes absconded from,
To know them new in tears and, later, smiles:

In love you prayed would linger long,
Would lift you up as strong as strong,
To gaze down on your gallous life,
That searing strife, the weatherglass unmoving
                       set for storms in you and me,
And nothing like a landscape you imagined you would see.

The Xanax and the Valium,
The alcohol and Librium:
Dystopias we wander from
To wander to again.
The weekdays and the tedium,
Impeccant hope grown weak and almost gone,
The sanctuaries we spurn when young
Till ageing turns our sun days into rage and rueful rain.

A haymaker to wake you, time will
Never tire, ignore you,
Never bowdlerise or bore you.
What you dreamed in youth to be your door
Has now turned out to be a floor,
And you fell facedown on that floor,
That filthy base,
To find your proper face,
Alone and down and done and none the wiser any more.
But yours of now as it was yours of yore.

There was a crooked person,
Who had walked a crooked mile.
And that was me. And that was you.
And where will we go now in wiser style?

If you suggest a venue,
I will be there in the hour.
Like a flower,
And, like a flower, grow. You know? The flowers grow. Despite
Our darkest efforts, there is springtime after winter,
Like the soft skin after scarring
After syringe and sharpest things and shard and splinter.

So I wonder, after all of this, is something sure awaiting
Round the bend that leads from hopelessness to holiness?
Where is the golden grail we toiled to tarnish?
Who makes the mindful music we were promised?
Where is the holy mothering, the beauty?
Where is the lifetime full of love and goodness come a duty?
If all of it has burned our way
And terrified our new grass into gorse,
If all of it has fled away,
If we have lapsed and veered astray,
Whatever could be worse?

Things could be worse:
The love you know will live on long and lift us strong and lean,
Beyond this lashing life, this searing strife, this war and more,
Will be the love you're hoping it can be: will endure.

O woman watching over
My bent shoulder as I write,
Look in me, holy haruspex,
And guide my thoughts, attend their flight.
Seer-channeller, sweet sorceress, my light,
Direct me: in these ways you are rehearsed
And better versed.
Now help me find the wording
And the ordering most right,
Augur well my auspex noble,
Guide my thoughts, attend their flight.
Seer-channeller, sweet sorceress,
                              my light, assuage this thirst:
Let breathing be our second language; poetry our first.

The people we were
And now are, and become,
May be broken, in need of repair,
But hope remains a fearsome flame too difficult to dowse,
Abides with us together in this little crooked house.

CARILLON (BEFORE CANDLES, AFTER DARK)

Grey svelte cloud-shadows hug copses and concretes,
Petulant breezes a-rattling the door.
Nothing of us in this bedlam of boundaries,
No countries or coast any more.
We reached our ripped and random
Borders geographical,
Venn-diagrammed, half-moving mass.
O twist us twinned and twined in tandem,
O leave us broken, brittler than before,
Marooned on scarred and shaky shifting shore.

To not profane this lovely life,
Be ambushed by our arrogance
Is all that we desire:
Our quest for something solider,
Our pipedreams of stability.
For closeness can save us
As distance does damage,
As life metes us madness
And mayhem to manage.

Battling like abandoned words
Towards some once poetic place,
And second guessing mascarpone
Cheesecake into metaphors,
The ghost come home is calm
And sews our days like reticella,
Tames and braids our noxious nights
Like angel hair, like bobbin lace.

All our guesswork, sketchiest,
Informs us we have erred:
Unobservant, deafened,
Nothing seen, and nothing heard.
All our love was wasted
Until all that could remain
Were tragedies oft-tasted,
All the flavours of our pain.

And I dream of Marco Polo,
Eyes alert, notating skies,
Describing bridges,
Unbuilt bridges
That will bear his name long after,
And later, quick to sleep, in sleep to roam,
Beneath a calmful coverlet of stars,
Soon dreaming of the seas and sailing home.

CATALPA

Until I'm breeding lilies
With my milk-white-shrouded mother
In our piece of moon-blanched sky,
I watch behind my window-mirror
Spent but restless not to rest:
Not tonight, my Josephine,
Not today, my Norma Jean,
For I am moving and my mind mists
Like red wine spilled on life's atlas,
Like devoré on dry dowlas:
Thus these mysteries, this foreignness,
This faith deferred, this lawlessness
Of love.

These Plexiglas electric
Sliding doors sigh so proleptic:
Mistook, anachronistic,
As our love is an error in time.
But we enter the cathedral,
Leave the rose garden behind.
To leave this life untarnished,
Pristine, polished, shining burnished
Requires a luckier star than this half-perished star of mine,
So it will never be. There is no time.
And I am sure of nothing
But the holiness of love, of love divine.

In a hot July, on Monday,
I tarried sun-roasted in Rome,
Beside the shining scaffolding
Atop the Spanish Steps,
And I wondered where you're gone to,
And I wondered how it is there,
And I wondered if they love you,
And I wondered how you are.

Arose and went and stood
Alone and cried in silent shaded solitude,
Inside the humble box-room

Where John Keats had lain
Two hundred years ago
Gasping for a god-sent breath,
Reaching for restoring Roman
Air that would not come and never came.

Stepping out in sunbeams once again,
I stole three mauve catalpa flowers
From Keats's tiny terrace rockery:
One for you, and one for me,
And one lest things be
Not as damaged or as darkling as my dying star,
As meaningless, forsaken,
Or as hopeless, unremembered,
Void or over as I've grown to think they are.

KINDLING

If winter winds
Must make you break
Your blue guitar

To use God's wood
For kindling, please
Give me a bell and let me haste

Before you bend and bust
And rend its noble frame,
So I can hear you strum

Your angel song
For one
Last precious time.

I love your song
Beyond myself
And cannot know a silence now

That wears a face I want. So
This is why and this is how
I come to be this thief I am

Bamboozled by fate's forests,
Breaking branches,
Making firewood,

And every twig and log and stick
I stack like hope outside your home
Before the frosts begin.

CLIMBABLE

Urn and bird and bard and star,
How I wonder what you are;
Scared I strum this scarred guitar:
How can sadness stretch her arms so far?
How can desolation stain so very very far?
Witnessed ends have been, have been, have been —
Autumnal glades we wished were evergreen,
This tawny titian fall once springtime vernal and pristine —
Prognosis, presage, portent, instance,
Imaged omen, symbolized scenario
Of Damoclean death. Accumulated sorrow slow amalgamates,
Agglomerates, regenerates our grievous wounds to webs
Of granulation. Makes a matrix, must repair, remain,
Reside in us like ribose, cassonade to
Calm and numb the nervous nucleus, survive in us
Like soothing sunset, softer scent,
Serener now, less vile, less vexed, less vast, less violent.

Inside my buckled blue cocoon
Mind pauses like an exile strayed a line too far,
Behoves me brake and re-embark,
Retrieve the little twinkling star,
Roam back to where the binding beauties are:
Violet snowbell soldanella,
Lath and plaster, beam and rafter,
Airy archipelago of love's disarming arabesque,
The dendrite that decrees itself a foliage alive.
Embers to ashes to cinder-soot fire,
Windowless walls and the language
Of flowers: this wild white-fringed orchid,
This palest egret, low and wistfully whispers:
'My soul will search down deaths and dreams for you.'

Dead sheep dress the downstream deluge,
Candid crumbling carcasses caressed by
Clement weather, clearer water. Halt, and ask,
What is their story? What is yours, and what is mine?
Tedious tutorials in terror taught by time until
We hear the tambourine above the tumult

Though this useless universe is upside down
And life needs neither petrol nor champagne,
Till something looms
And locksmith love unpicks a padlocked heart and lets you in.

Then the traveller in the dark,
Thanks you for your tiny spark,
He could not see which way to go.
I could not see which way to go.

Like nature you come flying fixing fractured fallen flowers,
Like wind-song you come whooshing
                              waking warm propitious powers,
Like sunrise you come shining
                              blessing storm-bent broken bowers,
Like daybreak you come dashing fetching hopeful honest hours.

So everything is opened. We can wander wide and far.
But best to linger longest where the binding beauties are:
This airy archipelago of love's disarming arabesque,
My solitary zinnia bloom, bring butterfly and breeze,
Life's less than sessile sylvan groves bear
Bosky beauty lined with unseen ageing
                              in the rings inside the trees;
And this is truth that hauls me all but heavenward,
Sectilic with epiphanies,
These signs sublime commune and chime, each
Elevates my tiptoed soul to sneak a peek anew
Like hungry hovering hummingbirds, up peeping
Through the darkling to the sparkling
To invert the lethal lysis, rouse the oxidizing part,
And renovate this ransacked room,
                              this raped and rundown ageing heart.

For everything has opened. We are wandering wide and far.
And best to linger longest where the binding beauties are:
O fulgent sun come fierce and bright,
It's thawing out the Argenite,
It's turning darkness into light,
Translating blindness into sight,
Transmuting silence into something right.
It's setting ashen cinder-soot alight,

It's silvering these edges of our clouds,
Could make of me a convert, a disciple,
A believer, and it has.

The hardest cross of steel and stone
Becomes the gentle cross of trust and tears.
The leaden bells become the silver bells
That tell you who you are and what to know and
How to heal and how to grow. So offer your good ear
To the mantic mouth of morning,
The romantic mouth of morning, hear
The madrigals, the melodies, the harmonies, the symphonies,
And know that you are loved and not alone.
Your angel is the orchid, pale egret:
Her soul will search down deaths and dreams for you.

As your bright and tiny spark,
Lights the traveller in the dark.
And I know now what you are,
And I know now where you are.

And know this news is meekly meant,
And hear this hymn so shyly sent:
You rise in skies to reinvent,
To slowly soar to glide content,
To softly skirr through firmament,
Glissade to scent, this joy unspent,
To smoothly steer, commenced descent,
To pilot true, dive understanding,
This cleared approach unturbulent,
And love will be the landing.

And finally the sheerest chines
Come climbable: each quest creates
A colophon to tell a troubled toiler, later,
How and why and where we had to travel after all:
To prove this pass is passable, this peak
A place of possibles and peace,
This mountain more than mountable,
This hill-rise hewn of Hope and Love
That can not, will not cease,
To sign the sky

To indicate the winding waking way,
As spring's right songbirds sing
And serenade and send again
A healing song, another yawning, dawning day.

THIS IS WHAT HAPPINESS LOOKS LIKE

How are we this august evening? How long is this line?
Who will dance through death's deep deluge?
                     Is this raging maelstrom really only mine?
What designed the friendly dendrite? Who is good to go?
How to navigate this nightscape, I will never know.

Where did you descend from, demon?
                   What makes you persist?
Who remains here hopeful after? Who cannot exist?
How to live as neat and new and young as next year's snow?
How your soul can shine circadian, I will never know.

How can we rebuild the refuge? Why must beauty die?
Why does not this faith succumb
                   and plummet from the lying sky?
How old will be old enough? How does your garden grow?
How to make the mountains murmur, I will never know.

When will life be stilled and stormless?
                   Saved and safe and sound,
Stepping over dragons as we leave the pillaged town,
Fancied that you whispered to me, love-words leal and low.
How you hold me, why you linger, I will never know.

HOME IN ONE

Should your ashes weigh more than the wings you once wore,
Your mercuric mad Icarus dream be no more,
Come on home. I am here. I will unlock the door
To the heights and the healing, once more you can soar.

One life more you can rise, mount the clouds, seek the sun,
Leave your fear of not flying, of deeds still undone;
Waxen plumage unmelted, God's crude cosmos outrun,
In your flight you will feel some fresh Hope is begun.

It will stir like old slumbering ogres disturbed,
It will purr with the tabbies and chirp with the birds,
Like the meanings of memories lift words lost for words,
It remains, to be clutched and re-loved, to be heard.

It shall shore up the shakiest stairways, spring clean,
It will spring a new start, transplant heart into spleen,
Delving, hidden, in debris, dead dust we have been;
Ashened lytic quicksilver, between to be seen.

It survives in new diamonds belief births from dust,
Like a river unfrozen, like this time-leavened lust,
It repairs over damage, reforms under rust,
It remains, to be clutched and re-loved, to be touched.

THE HISTORY OF OTHERING

In this infancy of ageing,
With its alchemies upstaging
All my vain attempts to tame time's tactile tide,
I set my dreams out wild and wide
As mad Canute's transparent dam:
I love, and I am loved, therefore I am, I am,

I am.

QUALIA

The greenness of the garden grass,
The pantile roofing red beside
The greying coast at Flamborough Head
That gifts us ginnelled coves to hide inside

Away from ironies, banana-skin fragilities.
The way things seem to want to be is fine,
Must keep us this way up, must liberate
The poetry from life when there is time.

The meltwater, the headland chalk,
The rugged shale, a seaboard shingle spit,
The sterner cliffs that jut and jut
And keep their peace and just get on with it.

LEVIATHAN

When all is lost and mangled
In a *mauvais foi* prosaic,
Or days kaleidoscopic, I shall
Seek a way to save it,

Must make my own mosaic
With my bonnetful of bees and
Ps and Qs. I will be watchful
As Leviathan, the lighthouseman.

This liminal life in a luminous house,
My sailor's gait heart and no spouse:
Sad things sent to try us from above,
And that is how you learn to lose your love.

O vigilant Leviathan,
I have to get it right from now:
The substance and the surfaces,
I want to find a window:

A karma sutra cognitive,
Of will, as of the willing flesh.
My doubting empire, watch me wounded,
Walking through the woken world undressed.

The sudden sexless skeleton of what was once ambition;
The murdering of memory, my mission:
The shadows of the night and the shadows of the day
Keep secrets same and different, hide things we cannot say.

The shadows of the day and the shadows of the night
Have much to do with angles, have much to do with light;
So superimposing yourself on this day,
You yearn for this; you wish for that. You half pretend to pray.

CHEKOV'S RIFLE

'My, people come and go so quickly here.'
(Dorothy, The Wizard of Oz)

You know exactly where you are and what you are tonight,
And listening to this sad demonic wind, this all seems right.
You know exactly who you are. You need no helping light.
You need no help. You need no one. You need no second sight.

So weep away, it rains and rains,
                    this streeted darkness grieves,
The shadows of dead pasts retreat
                            beneath the drooping eaves,
Beneath the ruined roofing, to the attic space like thieves,
This love so seldom seems to stay.
                        It leaves and leaves and leaves.

THE SECOND ARROW

Man: Have you been hurt?
Woman: What do you mean by hurt?
(Overheard at Piazza Rossetti, Vasto, Italy, 2014)

As yours can be the secret soul,
The lignite coal-gem glinting under coal,
This thinnest ice disc skated safely on:
Thin window to the deepest depths not gone,

But clear as crystal lakeland now,
May recent seasons wrap us up in rapture
After rapture of a joy we learn to capture
After nature's placid rhythms teach us how.

The second arrow always hurts
More than the first could ever do,
The second arrow hewn from grief, shot
Self-directed, deemed and done by you.

Oh breathe like Enid's silver breeze,
Protect our fragile paradise,
Be prescient, find futures safe to seize,
Be one with all these arrows and this ice.

YUKIMARIMO (JERUSALEM TO JERICHO)

The Good Samaritan came by, and he reversed the question:
"If I do not stop to help this man, what will happen to him?"'
(Martin Luther King)

Lamed over lowlands my limbs sink like stones.
Stranger, Levantine, support me.
Dark are my Bible dreams, bruised my black bones,
Resting where questing has brought me.

Lonely are we who love leaving too much,
Trapped in departure, past frozen:
Colder than cobalt, blue flowers we clutch,
Old in our colours ill chosen.

High on her hill sleeps my silent princess,
Mute for the prince made to miss her;
Waken her soft, melt her hoarfrosted lips.
Carry me up there to kiss her.

NOT NOW

Oh, somewhere in this favoured land the sun is shining bright,
A band soft serenading near, love sings a heart so light,
For life's a big pink whirligig, our magic roundabout,
And somewhere men are laughing loud,
                              and somewhere children shout.

My whitest water hyacinth, so like my drifting days,
You do not know you have no root to anchor you. This maze
Can be our Eden if we wish, life's gyroscopic gift;
And yet we bob and float where currents drag us,
                                    dead we drift.

PLAGAL CADENCE

In the preludes of probable places,
In the dawn of degrees of belief,
I still witness their forms and their faces:
Olden ghostings, but blissfully brief.

I wander past the ruins where
The hatchling birds cry hopeful hymns.
Awonder with the wintry winds,
I close my eyes to keep these visions in.

PROVENIENCE

My wellspring wells and wets and moistens me
Despite these recent deftest cruel encroaching drags of
Dryness. These duller dismal grown-up deeds I have
To do usurp my life like highwaymen or highway girls,

Can snatch and grab the things I want to do.
I want to stay alive and here and home with you.
I have to have to, too.
                    Atop the juice this pair of songbirds kilter
Wildly, gambol high, dawn's briskest reunited Gemini,

In elegance archaic, in a simple sky,
Outpacing the prosaic, in a single sky.

KLEOS

Words we need for loving well are
Limited and barer fare
Than words we'll need for leaving,
Loud and palpable, not rare.

Words we use thereafter will be
Gentler than vile violent verbs
We javelin back when partings black
Our ways of predicating bliss: our war of words.

Words we wait too long to hear are
Obvious as seasons yet they pounce full pelt
Like winter winds announcing snows we
Pray will fall then pray will never melt.

Words we'll long to leave behind will make
It worth our while to linger, though they say
The wall of words we need for loving
Well has stood too long. Has worn away.

SONNET

Should these my blessed idle eyes
Surprise me? Yes they should and sure
They do. I can believe my open eyes.
I can but trust this wobbly paradise
That keeps me coming back
To covet love like stolen smiles
Or glimpse thereof with other
Soulless would-be spies:

Has me mistaking azure
Moods for skies and all the faith
That soars above sub-astral lies.
That flies like birds of paradise,
And flies and flies and never dies:
Surprise, surprise. Surprise.

SISYPHUS (IMPIOUS KING OF CORINTH)

(to his wife Merope, star-nymph Pleiad of Corinth)

A fortune I have failed to own
Is yours as flames belong to fire;
In company or crowds, alone,
Your living light best bids the dark retire.

A treasure I had fished to find
In storm-smashed oceanic time
Swims seas serene that you designed
And rises like a perfect rippling rhyme.

These riches I can't cease to crave
Are found, are all around, are here;
Your lambent love, spangled to save,
That thaws like suns. That does not disappear.

SHEER

The courtesy of metaphor:
Red rose, you are not Love. You stray,
Mere flower, as clearest skies

Grow grey or rose or dark like days, but stay
Our welkin. What quiesced us once
Can calm anew: all shades we see will be.

You see: I am the sky and
So are you. Do not blush blue (but if
You wish to, do). Sheer, liminal as chiffon dew,

You alter with the light like colours do;
Love's achromatic rose holds, waits for hue;
My blank and gessoed canvas waits for you.

LADY NEWING NATURE &
THE GHOSTS OF LASTING LOVE

The Ghosts of Lasting Love have left
For good, as ghosts have fled before.
Embracing that quixotic lack,
The champagned bath we linger for

Will cleanse the pilgrim soul that gives
As Lady Newing Nature gives: Her sun
For least-expecting, least-deserving me and you,
Her sumptuous summer flowerings begun.

AND LOVE WILL BE THE LANDING

(A quartet of previously unpublished poems
inspired by 'Interrupted Landing',
a multi-media collaboration with Susan Mowatt,
Davy Henderson, and Hidetoshi Tomiyama,
based around some poems from Homing by Paul Hullah (2011),
that resulted in artworks exhibited and performed
in Japan and Scotland during 2012.

These poems were not included in the text of 'Interrupted Landing'.
Rather, they are my own interpretations of
what we made and did in that piece.)

1. EARTHED

Muses ascending steep stairs to our bower,
Rising in white and in blue;
In Purity's colour,
In Memory's hue:
The sage silent sisters, sheer sibyls
In silkaline, seers melt the madness for you.

Ably predicting the dreadful departures,
Direst for lives that remain,
Left mulling in golden
Warm orchards, green plains,
The blameless spring landmasses stretching
Arched, careful as wakening cats, right as rain.

Symbols still shimmer to signify stasis,
Shadows, not stories, come true.
My symbols sing softly
Of Pureness anew,
And Memory, mending and merging
These journeys: of me, of this soil, and of you.

Outside our discomfort zone, so no longer
Re-interrupted by pain,
Re-birthed and re-earthed now,
We see desire plain.
Lined landscape of lack turned to teacher
Of ways to repair, wake the world up again.

Halt here, close listen to love's closing lesson;
Hearken to hope's wise old land.
Re-centred and sober,
Shape loam with sure hands,
Build your last abode, find foundations
On firmest terrain. Welcome home. Understand.

2. HOME

Days we stayed alive for make us new; blaze in
More buoyant now with Muses gushing music much untouched
By sadness, loss, and lonesome dusk. We are the winners
Here. We woke, to find a future, to begin.

Chosen sibling victor, gentle leader: here you are. Hand
Me down my walking shoes and let me leave
With you. I want to walk with you. We may not move too far,
But we shall see so much.
　　　　　　　　When we have learned to like this land-

-marked life we'll be at home. You do not know
What happened here; I do, so I have
Set it down. We slither round reality, waste love and time
With every lowly lapse.
　　　　　　　　We stumble, fall; we rise, we go, we grow.

That quiet we don't know now keeps us talking;
Rarest hillsides, ripest havens, we would go
Up there, be mended, wounded walking,
Reminded of the silence we don't know.

Years we stayed asleep for do not matter now. We
Erred, but that is over. We can carve a clearer channel, clear
A better way. Gaze ahead, this view is free:
You live to learn these lines, to get from here to here, to be.

3. LANDING

We were interrupted. What has happened here? Where are all the symbols and the scriptures that we wished on? Which days of this life will we remember most, or speak of least, not miss like never pined for aches and anxious pangs? Where go all our favourite days? Where are starlit eves we carolled into dawn's good blue? Who are friends we never knew, and where are friends we lost? Who will be the next one? When will it be over or begin? How can we move forward through this maelstrom of mortality? Where is home, the unimagined image? How do we get in?

The journeying is populous with obstacles; poor progress paved with pitfalls. We find ourselves impeded, slowed, obstructed, made to wait. A line can trace a road or mark a boundary; can sign to us to stop, or urge us to go on. All importance rests in choice, so we can take control, design our own route forward, steer a course for home. When we know how to choose, we will value our voyages fully. We will come to appreciate arrival more.

Everything goes from one place to another, and every connection is also a departure. Like the lines on the land a tractor's tyres draw, skate trails on ice, the furrows in turf that a pushed plough will make: saying I was here, but I was on my way to somewhere else as well. Like everything we utter, all we do. We have left proof, evidence, marks of our selves as we travel in space and in time, as we will leave this 'here' for someplace new, a land as yet unlined, untravelled routes, a sky as yet unseen.

So we live to keep living and we look to keep learning. Shadows show us substance; silence sings us song. We see shapes in the sky; in the mayhem we make meaning. Through chaos we come to know order; by darkness we come to know light. These are the lines on the land. This is the homing we hope for and, hopefully, finally find. Look at the streets full of colour, the birds in the trees, the furrowed new fields, those small children, these crystal clear canals of time, these moments when the future looms like lights. That is what we're here for. That is what we wake for, want for, work for, wish for. What else will ever matter?

These memories make us, and so we come back to them. While the house is occupied with sounds or later deeply sleeping, we sneak unseen outside to breathe the vaster air. This land is now home. There is a soothing separate kind of silence here. You can sense a gentler hush beneath the dawn's bright jangling birdsong, and the starlit nights are perfect. There is no way of knowing surely, but sometimes you think you can guess what people want to mean even if they're strangers you have never met before. We can put the parts together; mix the memories with moments that we meld with as we move. And even when we're wrong, it's more than nothing. It is always something new.

So let love in like light through your bulky blackout drapes. Let it have you, let it hit you, let it hurt you, let it hold you, let it heal you. Choose to start the world again; you always can. The truth will wait to find you, will amaze you, its goodness leave you dumbstruck at its magic almost holy splendour. That goodness is love; that truth is built on love. Love will render all the rest worthwhile. Love will be the thing that disappoints you least in life. After all the interrupted landings comes the one that brings you home. There is meaning in the healing; there are maps amidst the chaos, landmarks on the rough terrain, latent lucent linings in the darkest fogs of loss. There is a way, a road, a thoroughfare. There is a way home. After the sadness and the madness comes the learning, comes the landing, comes the image unimagined, comes the love. And love will be the landing.

4. THE GATE

Our foreseeable past was in hindsight
Transparent with light;
But we took
It for darkness, mistook
It for night. For something
Went wrong that was right.

Less is more. The more
We write the smaller things or
Words become. The prospect
Of joy chimes like clocks in the dark, vivid, vast;
Till never being lonely looks
Achievable at last.

So rise like roots from turgid tundra:
Free our selves anew.
Stretch like roads, like lined terrain;
Home will be here. Love lives near to you

And lets this life loll on, takes time, makes space,
Lets fertile fields and gardens grow apace.
We leave the gloom behind, fly forth, embrace,
Locate the gate called Beautiful, (this place),
The kindness in that face, this giving grace.

FOR HER SAKE

You will walk this town, your roaming on,
Summering snugly and wintering well,
Sprung and fallen into hope that holds
Your heart up like a shouldered funfair child,
Wanting to see, pushed aloft to do so.
This strangest ease,
Post-modern anti-life,
Peels back like blistered paint.
Walk inland from the harbour's edge
And head for home and know she will be there.
Repealed, repair; reposed, repair.
Do all this not for your sake but for hers.

And do this for your world's sake, make it mean
Like rain on sun-baked sand, always wanted, all but
Sucked from air like goodness out of loss.

Bereft we wait all year for rain,
As Icarus dances. The mercury rises again.

INSIDE

Inside a night I cannot name,
Inside a darkness deepest not in days, but down in me,
I looked for light, some spark, a holy flame;
I found it in a love I now can see.

Outside a cage I left alone
There is a green hill glad with golden gorse in bloom anew:
There I abide, quelled by your mind, at home,
Inside a sunlit safehouse named for you.

THE TITLE OF THIS TIME

Is joyance. Winter fears fugacious here
Cease softly to pertain, as pristine, fragile, sheer

Sun-spangled cryptic memo snowflakes fall,
Settling scripted solace from a kindly sky. All

Comes so clear, cleansed world canescent. See,
Perhaps this can be poetry:

White snowflakes on a whitened day,
On lifted life, meant well, well meant to stay.

O SADNESS

O sadness, you sneak thief, you stole
All my homes, turned my hurt soul
Nomadic, nocturnal, not whole
Any more. No words to console

My torn ventricles now:
All my valves are kaput. How
They leak all my lustre, allow
Darkness to enter. O sadness, your vow

Was to show me the ways
Of the world, and you did. Days
Come black, cannot unsee this violent night.
I find neither foothold nor homeland nor light.

THE WAKING RIVER

In drowsing dawns I dare to hope will break
You are the waking river, run so
Deep, far deeply stiller than my hectic
Heart; come clearer than the seasons' pass-
Age, fluent for the future, meet for mine.

In music you mass words in me to make
You are the sure composer, come to
Give this day your genius like water
Between barren banks, beneath this moiling
Light, whence now begins a beauty;
Rouse, my river. Start, my song.

AGAIN

'What looks large from a distance, close up ain't never that big.'
(Bob Dylan, 'Tight Connection To My Heart')

Going slower, going older,
Expanding what were grey
Zipped files of my rushed life
Before into a newer view, a way

Of seeing stubborn goodness
That was always there
And means I won't be lonely here again
Or anywhere.

Me and my subjunctives
My lamentable trends;
You had to be there. So you were.
As you see fit, proceed. I'll make amends.

The daily forecasts always wrong:
The skies are lies as they
Leave blue for grey, as people change.
So where I am I to go now? Where am I to stay?

To newer doors, you smile
Like suns and gently say,
And all the weathers walk away.
And all the terrors peel away

From me and that shocked boy
Who once cried wolf, then cried
Some words that no one else could hear,
And then just cried and cried and cried.

ROMAN Á CLEF

As if you knew,
As if the sky was telling you,
As if the blue was yours, your blue;
As if you knew.

As if you do,
As if you do these things for you,
And not for anyone but you;
As if you do.

As if it's true,
That spectre in the sky, still watching you,
Has never taken care of you;
It is not true.

STARTED

'Are you starting?' (3AM passer by, Great Junction Street, Edinburgh, 2015)

'I am started. The tugs have left me.' (Wilfred Owen)

Indecorous and riven, I dredge
Riverbeds, my melted dreams, no centre here, no edge.

How best to live a grounded life, abscond
From teacup storms and mediocre faith? Beyond

The simple elegance of knowing this
Is what remains, those Vestal skies are hope and home I miss.

Vestiges in embers of what went before,
My ashes weigh more than the wings I once wore.

RIBBONS I RISE IN ARE RIBBONS I REST IN

I don't know where to hear her voice,
And so I dredge my darkest dreams,
These fairy tales for fallen men,
Till solace speaks through smithereens.

To know again the gladdest thing
We must revisit everything:
The turgid days and perfect days,
The quarries full of gems and full of waste.

CRUSOE

Should shades of sadness stalk you
To the seashore of the island loss you keep;
Locate a ship-shaped swim-hole in the saving sea
And dive down deep and deep.

Should restless skies of rancour stop your view,
Remind you how to wane and weep;
Locate a bed-shaped break between black clouds
And go to sleep, and sleep.

Should you surmise that you are grounded still,
Look for light and luck that lets you leap;
Locate a home, a happy ending here,
And keep, and keep, and keep.

BETROTHED

If all Pan's singing pilgrims have
A good song in them somewhere,
Maybe I am not mistaken: maybe some of this is mine?

This broken buckled soul at last
Betrothed to hopes of homing, whole again
Like shifted silt from silent sea-floor streams,

No more enraged by age, engaged by rages
Of regression into versions of the void
That went before. So seldom lost or lonely any more?

The ghost at the wheel
Of my getaway heart sings a song
I have heard in the stones of the closes

And ginnels and wynds of this city:
Your melody remembered, as the Stockbridge
Swallows speculate on southern skies in June.

As ballerinas sense a scuffed shellac
Beneath the graceful *grand jeté*, I sense
A fierce phalanx of frightening futures,

Trickster tugs of trite respite
That plays pretender to relief. I glimpse
The guilty grief behind the lifting lights,

A night moon mirrored on the tarry brine
In negative, your holy eye, imploring
Me arise from inward shadows,
                motion now to mount and climb

The near and believable star-lane, ascending lit ladder above:
Most faithful of friends I have
Kept in my heart and have never forgotten to love.

And if you ask how I regret that parting?
It is like the flowers falling at spring's end, confused, whirled in a tangle.
What is the use of talking! And there is no end of talking —
There is no end of things in the heart.
(Ezra Pound, 'Exile's Letter')